To. . . . .
For being good.
MERRY CHRISTMAS!
From

It was a crisp Christmas Eve
and Santa and his reindeers
were busy delivering presents to
all the good boys and girls.

Santa's sleigh zoomed over houses, twisting
and turning silently through the snowy night sky.
Santa squeezed down and up and up and down
chimneys, carefully and quietly delivering
lots of presents.

All was going to plan until he reached the second to last house on his list.

Suddenly, Santa noticed one of the presents was **missing**!

The reindeer looked in Santa's sack, they **searched everywhere** but the present was nowhere to be found!

"Oh no!" exclaimed Santa. "It must have fallen off the **sleigh**!"

Santa wondered what to do.
He had no time to look for the present but he didn't want to disappoint anyone on his Christmas list.

Then Santa had a **FANTASTIC** idea!

He looked at his delivery map to see where they were.
Then he checked his list to see who had been naughty or nice.

At the very
top of the list was Archer.........
So Santa and Blitzen (the smallest of
all the reindeer) squeezed
down the chimney...

...and crept quietly into her bedroom.

. . . . yawned, stretched and rubbed her eyes. She thought she was still **dreaming** until Blitzen licked her face with his long, wet, pink tongue – **YUCK!**

"I need your help!" boomed Santa. He explained that a present had fallen off the sleigh and Santa wanted Archer to go with Blitzen to find it.

Archer... of course was VERY happy to help.

It was cold and snowy outside so . . . .
put on her warmest
hat and long,
stripy scarf.

. . . .
and Blitzen
looked through
Santa's telescope.

They looked down past the
houses and through the trees,
trying to find the lost present.

Suddenly they spotted it,
sitting on top of a pile of snow
at the bottom of a big hill.

She jumped on Blitzen's back and gave him
a friendly pat and little tickle
behind his fluffy ears.
Then with a gentle nudge they flew
high into the starry night sky.

Up and up they soared

higher and higher

until Blitzen did a
loop the loop,
a flip and a flop
and landed with a bop
next to the pile of snow...

but the present had gone!

. . . . and Blitzen looked around but couldn't see the present **anywhere**!

All of a sudden Blitzen's wet nose began to twitch and itch and wibble and wobble. What had he found?

. . . . saw a bright orange carrot sticking out of the snow. "Who likes carrots?" she wondered. Perhaps this was a clue to where the present had gone.

Then they saw a tiny white and grey bunny rabbit.

"Hello Mrs Rabbit, we're **looking** for a missing gift which fell from Santa's sleigh. Have you seen **anything**?"

The bunny **twitched** her nose, rubbed her ears and **pointed** a fluffy white paw at a line of acorns.

"Who likes acorns?"
wondered
. . . .

Then looking down, they noticed a
bouncy red squirrel staring back at them.
They followed him, picking up the acorns one by one,
not knowing who or what would be at the end of the trail.

As they picked up the final acorn, they noticed a nose-less, button-less, very sad snowman right in front of them.

His carrot nose had fallen off and his acorn buttons had been lost but there, poking out from under his black hat, was a shiny Christmas present!

Hurray, they had found the present...
but why did the snowman have it?

The sad snowman explained that every year he felt forgotten as he never received a present. When he found this one he was so happy. However, now he knew it belonged to someone else, he wanted to give it back.

Feeling sorry for the snowman,
. . . . decided to help.
She placed the half-eaten carrot
on the snowman's face for his nose
and the acorn buttons on his body
but the snowman still looked sad.

Then . . . .
had a brilliant idea!

She undid her **fluffy** scarf and tied it around the surprised snowman.

Then she replaced the snowman's old black hat with her warm knitted one.

The snowman was so **happy!** At last he had his very **OWN** Christmas present!

. . . . and Blitzen flew as fast as they could to get the missing present back in time for **Christmas** morning.

. . . . placed the gift under the tree with a **huge** sigh of relief!

Back at home . . . . gave Blitzen a **big hug**, then watched as her new friend flew up into the sky and home to Santa.

When . . . .
woke up on
Christmas morning,
she wondered if it
had all been a dream.
Then she looked out
of her window...

...and there in the
distance was the happy
snowman waving at
her and he was still
wearing his lovely
Christmas present.

The end